THE
SCOTTSBORO
BOYS

BY DUCHESS HARRIS, JD, PHD
WITH TOM HEAD

Core Library

Cover image: The Scottsboro Boys were arrested on
March 25, 1931.

An Imprint of Abdo Publishing
abdobooks.com

abdocorelibrary.com

Published by Abdo Publishing, a division of ABDO, PO Box 398166,
Minneapolis, Minnesota 55439. Copyright © 2019 by Abdo Consulting
Group, Inc. International copyrights reserved in all countries. No part of this
book may be reproduced in any form without written permission from the
publisher. Core Library™ is a trademark and logo of Abdo Publishing.

Printed in the United States of America, North Mankato, Minnesota
092018
012019

Cover Photo: Bettmann/Getty Images
Interior Photos: Bettmann/Getty Images, 1, 26–27; UPPA/Photoshot/Newscom, 5, 43; CSU
Archives/Everett Collection/Newscom, 6–7; Buyenlarge/Getty Images, 9; Everett Collection/
Newscom, 11, 17; John Vachon/Library of Congress, 14–15; AP Images, 20–21, 28, 31; Red Line
Editorial, 30, 39; Bob Gathany/al.com/AP Images, 34–35; Lisa DeJong/The Plain Dealer/AP Images,
37; Michael Nigro/Sipa USA/AP Images, 40

Editor: Maddie Spalding
Series Designer: Claire Vanden Branden

Library of Congress Control Number: 2018949706

Publisher's Cataloging-in-Publication Data

Names: Harris, Duchess, author. | Head, Tom, author.
Title: The Scottsboro boys / by Duchess Harris and Tom Head.
Description: Minneapolis, Minnesota : Abdo Publishing, 2019 | Series: Freedom's
    promise | Includes online resources and index.
Identifiers: ISBN 9781532117756 (lib. bdg.) | ISBN 9781641856096 (pbk) | ISBN 9781532170614
    (ebook)
Subjects: LCSH: Scottsboro Trial, Scottsboro, Ala., 1931--Juvenile literature. |
    Right to a fair trial--Juvenile literature. | Trials (Rape)--Alabama--Juvenile
    literature. | Race prejudice--Juvenile literature.
Classification: DDC 345.7619502523--dc23

CONTENTS

A LETTER FROM DUCHESS

I went to law school to learn about justice. When I graduated, the commencement speaker spoke about *To Kill A Mockingbird*. She did not realize that this award-winning novel was based on the Scottsboro Boys trials. Instead of talking about the tragic lives of these young black boys who were victims of racism, she spoke about the legal skills of the book's white lawyer character.

It is important to understand what life was really like for black Americans in the South in the 1930s. They faced deep racism in all parts of daily life. This history is closely tied with the US justice system. The story of the Scottsboro Boys is a key example of that. Without this history, it is difficult to understand why the United States is the only nation with laws allowing life sentences for juveniles.

This book is about an event that many people have forgotten. I have tried to explain how the story of the Scottsboro Boys connects to US history and why it is important today. Join me on a journey that examines the promise of freedom.

Duchess Harris

The nine Scottsboro Boys meet with their lawyer in 1933.

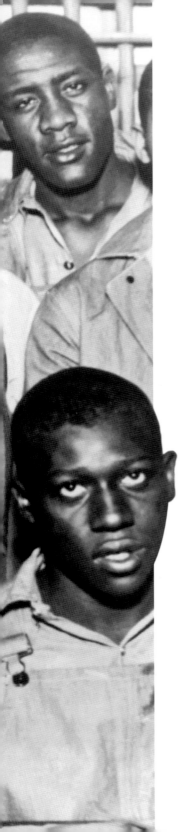

WRONGLY ACCUSED

A mob of men gathered in Paint Rock, Alabama. It was the afternoon of March 25, 1931. The sheriff had ordered his deputy to round up every armed white man he could find. Some men had sticks. Others held guns. Their orders were clear. They were to wait for a train arriving at the Paint Rock station. Then they were to arrest any black people on board.

The mob arrested nine black teenagers. Their names were Olen Montgomery, Clarence Norris, Haywood Patterson, Ozie Powell, Willie Roberson, Charles Weems, Eugene Williams, Andy Wright, and Roy Wright. The mob tied

The Scottsboro Boys ranged in age from 13 to 19 years old.

the young men together with rope and pushed them into a truck. They took the young men to a jail in nearby Scottsboro, Alabama. The men were charged with assault and attempted murder. These were false charges. The men had been attacked by a group of white teenagers on the train. They fought back in self-defense. But because of the color of their skin, law enforcement officers didn't ask for their side of the story.

By nightfall the young men had also been falsely accused of rape. The news spread in Scottsboro. A crowd soon gathered outside the jail. The crowd shouted and demanded justice. In the South, mob justice against a black person accused of a crime didn't include a fair trial. It often meant death.

For their safety, the young men were secretly moved from the Scottsboro jail to a jail in the nearby town of Gadsden, Alabama. The men huddled in jail cells for two weeks while awaiting their trials. Most of

In the 1930s, black people had to use separate facilities, such as drinking fountains.

them had not known each other before their arrest. But after their arrest, they would all be known together as the Scottsboro Boys.

LYNCH LAW

By 1931 slavery had been illegal in the United States for 66 years. Alabama had not banned slavery by choice. As part of the Confederacy, Alabama had

LYNCHING IN THE UNITED STATES

Researchers at the Tuskegee Institute found evidence that 4,743 people were lynched in the United States between 1882 and 1968. But there may have been many more. Some lynchings may not have been documented. Of the known lynchings, 347 took place in Alabama. Most lynching victims were African American. Other people of color were sometimes lynched as well.

defended slavery. The Confederacy lost the Civil War (1861–1865). This brought an end to slavery. But after the war, white politicians passed laws called Jim Crow laws. These laws made racial segregation legal in the South. Black people in Jim Crow Alabama were kept separate from white people. They could not occupy the same public spaces, such as restaurants.

Another way Alabama's government controlled black people was by letting white people murder them. White people in Alabama and throughout the South gathered in groups. They hunted down and murdered black people. These murders were called lynchings.

The National Association for the Advancement of Colored People used flags to draw attention to lynchings in the 1930s.

Law enforcement officers in the South rarely arrested people for lynchings. In fact, officers often helped commit lynchings. Some members of the US Congress tried to ban lynching, but they failed. Southern senators wanted to leave the issue to the states.

Between 1882 and 1930, approximately 2,828 people were lynched in the South. The Scottsboro Boys knew the accusations against them could cost them their lives. Their innocence alone would not protect them.

JIM CROW JUSTICE

The US Constitution protects a person's right to a fair trial. But black defendants in the Jim Crow South did not receive fair trials. They were rarely able to afford lawyers. They faced angry judges and all-white juries. Executions were used to satisfy angry mobs.

If they had not gone to jail, the Scottsboro Boys may have been killed by a lynch mob. But in jail, they faced an unfair criminal justice system. Few could have predicted that their trials would be among the first legal victories of the civil rights movement.

PERSPECTIVES

IDA B. WELLS

On the same day the Scottsboro Boys were arrested, journalist and civil rights activist Ida B. Wells died in Chicago, Illinois. Wells was among the first journalists in the United States to document lynchings. She began to write about lynchings after three of her friends were lynched in Memphis, Tennessee, in 1892. Her lynching investigations soon became her life's work. Wells's writings made apparent how widespread lynching was. Wells wrote in 1892 that "the way to right wrongs is to turn the light of truth upon them."

STRAIGHT TO THE
SOURCE

An article in the newspaper the *Daily Clarion-Ledger* documented the events that occurred on the night of March 25, 1931. The reporter explained the threats the Scottsboro Boys faced:

> *Feeling was intense here last night as mountaineers from throughout this section came trooping into town, some in automobiles and a few on mules. At times the crowd was estimated to number three hundred and a few times there were shouts of "lynch them."*
>
> *Inside the jail, Sheriff M. L. Wann, nine deputy sheriffs, and as many citizen volunteers, armed with shotguns, kept watch and warned the jostling men outside that they would shoot at the first attempt to rush the jail.*
>
> Source: "Move Accused Blacks Under Armed Patrol." *The Daily Clarion-Ledger.* Newspapers.com, March 26, 1931. Web. Accessed June 7, 2018.

Consider Your Audience

Adapt this passage for a different audience, such as your teacher or your friends. Write a blog post conveying the same information for this new audience. How does your post differ from the original text and why?

A WHITE MAN'S TRAIN

The nine Scottsboro Boys were all teenagers at the time of their arrest. The youngest of them, Eugene Williams and Roy Wright, were 13 years old. Andy Wright, Weems, and Norris were the oldest men in the group. They were each 19 years old. Most of the young men had hopped on the train in Georgia. Roy and Andy had boarded the train in Tennessee. The Wright brothers were traveling with Andy's two friends, Williams and 18-year-old Patterson. None of the other young men knew each other.

Many people boarded trains illegally during the Great Depression.

FREIGHT HOPPERS

In 1933 the *Wall Street Journal* reported that approximately half a million people illegally rode trains. These people were sometimes called freight hoppers. Most freight hoppers were younger than 25 years old. Security guards often threw black freight hoppers off of trains. But they usually ignored white freight hoppers.

The train was bound for Memphis, Tennessee. Most of the young men hoped to find jobs in Memphis. The Great Depression had hit many families hard. Most Americans were very poor. Work was hard to find. Trains ran across the country every day. These trains carried supplies for businesses. Some people who couldn't find jobs in their hometowns decided to ride these trains illegally. They tried to board without anyone noticing so they could ride for free. Trains brought them to other parts of the country, where they hoped to find work.

Patterson had been riding trains for four years, searching for work in different parts of the country. The Wright brothers hoped to find good jobs so they

Many people began working at a young age during the Great Depression to help support their families.

could earn enough money to support their mother in Tennessee. Sixteen-year-old Powell hoped to find a job as a lumber worker. Seventeen-year-old Montgomery wanted to earn enough money to buy a new pair of glasses.

THE FIGHT

The train was passing through northern Alabama when a fight broke out between the black teenagers and a group of young white men. One of the men stepped on Patterson's hand. The man began to argue with Patterson. He said that Patterson and the other black men didn't belong on the train. The train slowed, and the white men hopped off. They picked up gravel and threw it at the black men on the train. Then the white men jumped back on. The fight continued in the train car. The black men joined together to defend themselves against the white men. The black men managed to throw the white men off the train in Stevenson, Alabama.

The white men found a man who worked at the Stevenson train station. They reported their side of the story. They described the black men as a gang. The station worker called officials in Paint Rock, where the train was due to stop next. Then a large group of white men gathered to pull the black men off the train in Paint Rock.

PRICE AND BATES

Two white women were also riding the train illegally that day. Twenty-one-year-old Victoria Price and 17-year-old Ruby Bates were headed to Chattanooga, Tennessee, to find jobs. When the train stopped in Paint Rock, Bates and Price feared they would be charged for riding the rails illegally. They made up a story to draw attention from themselves. They said that the nine black men had raped them. The Scottsboro Boys had not even seen the young women on the train. This false accusation would lead to years in jail and in court for the Scottsboro Boys. Their troubles were just beginning.

PERSPECTIVES

ROY WRIGHT

Roy Wright wrote to his mother while in an Alabama jail awaiting trial in June 1931. In his letter, he told her: "I feel like I can eat some of your cooking Mom. . . . Please don't write or tell me anything to make me feel good." He invited her to the prison but knew that visiting him would be hard for her. "You don't have to come," he wrote, "because I have your picture and I can look at it."

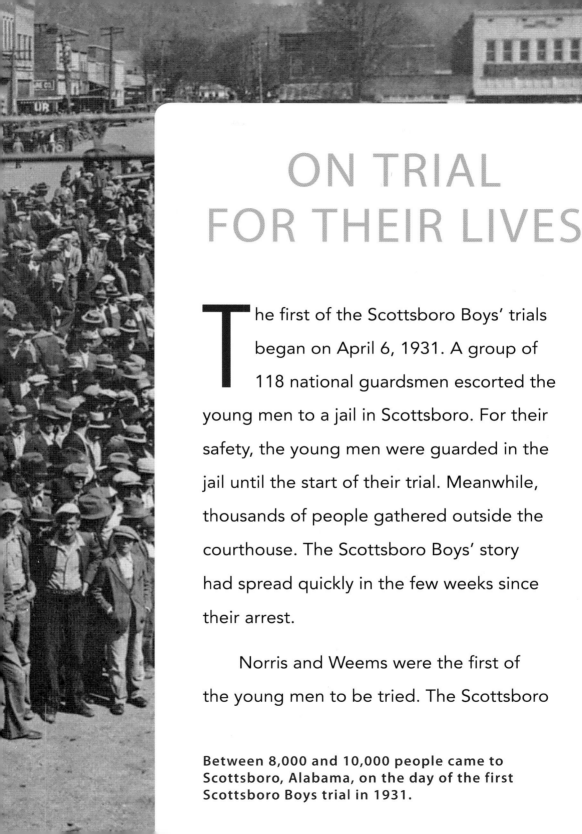

ON TRIAL FOR THEIR LIVES

The first of the Scottsboro Boys' trials began on April 6, 1931. A group of 118 national guardsmen escorted the young men to a jail in Scottsboro. For their safety, the young men were guarded in the jail until the start of their trial. Meanwhile, thousands of people gathered outside the courthouse. The Scottsboro Boys' story had spread quickly in the few weeks since their arrest.

Norris and Weems were the first of the young men to be tried. The Scottsboro

Between 8,000 and 10,000 people came to Scottsboro, Alabama, on the day of the first Scottsboro Boys trial in 1931.

defendants were not allowed to talk to their lawyer. This made planning their defense impossible.

The Scottsboro Boys were assigned a lawyer named Stephen Roddy. Roddy came from Chattanooga. He was not licensed to practice law in Alabama. He normally handled real estate cases, not criminal cases. He was also an alcoholic. He showed up to the trial drunk. He couldn't even walk straight.

Price and Bates testified in the trial. They stuck to the story that they had been raped. The all-white jury sentenced Norris and Weems to death. Trials for the rest of the young men quickly followed. By April 9, the court had handed down sentences for all of the Scottsboro Boys. All-white juries sentenced eight of them to death. Roy Wright was given a different sentence. Roy was the youngest of the Scottsboro Boys. Most of the jurors wanted to execute him. But the prosecutor did not want to execute someone so young. For this reason, his sentence was reduced to life in prison.

Officials beat and threatened the Scottsboro Boys. They used these tactics to force the young men to confess or turn on each other. The deputy sheriff and the judge whipped Roy. Under threat of further punishment, Roy testified against Norris and Weems. He said that he had seen Norris and Weems with Price and Bates on the train. Intimidation tactics also influenced Norris's testimony. Prison guards had told the Scottsboro Boys that if they didn't confess, the guards would give them to the mobs outside the jail.

PERSPECTIVES
KILBY PRISON

The Scottsboro Boys were moved to different prisons in the 1930s. One of these prisons was Kilby Prison in Montgomery, Alabama. The young men were kept there while on death row. Norris later recalled the living conditions at the prison. He said: "When you were allowed to take a shower, there would be two guards standing there as you left your cell, naked—one with a stick and the other with a gun. They would march you to the bathroom for a three- or four-minute shower."

Norris feared for his life. So he said that the other young men had committed rape.

FINDING ALLIES

Newspapers soon began to hear about the Scottsboro Boys' story. National civil rights organizations began calling for new and fairer trials. The National Association for the Advancement of Colored People (NAACP) offered its support. The International Labor Defense (ILD) also joined the cause. Together these organizations appealed the Scottsboro Boys' cases. This meant that a higher court would be able to review the verdicts. A higher court could change the young men's sentences.

STRAIGHT TO THE
SOURCE

Roy Wright was called to testify during Patterson's trial in early April 1931. Roy later recalled how officials hurt him until he agreed to testify against Norris and Weems:

> I was sitting in a chair in front of the judge and one of those girls [Price or Bates] was testifying. . . . Then the trial stopped awhile and the deputy sheriff beckoned to me to come out into another room—the room back of the place where the judge was sitting—and I went. They whipped me and it seemed like they was going to kill me. All the time they kept saying, "Now will you tell?" and finally it seemed like I couldn't stand no more and I said yes. Then I went back into the courtroom and they put me up on the chair in front of the judge and began asking a lot of questions, and I said I had seen Charlie Weems and Clarence Norris with the white girls.

Source: James Goodman. *Stories of Scottsboro*. New York: Pantheon, 1994. Print. 97.

What's the Big Idea?

Take a close look at this passage. Consider Roy Wright's age during the Scottsboro Boys' trials. Why do you think officials targeted Roy in this way? How might they have targeted the older Scottsboro Boys in different ways?

CHAPTER FOUR

APPEALS TRIALS

The ILD hired experienced lawyers to defend the Scottsboro Boys during their appeals trials. The first appeal was to the Alabama Supreme Court in January 1932. The ILD lawyers argued that the Scottsboro Boys had been judged unfairly because there had been only white people on the jury.

The Alabama Supreme Court made its ruling in March 1932. It ruled that seven of the eight death sentences were fair. The court said the state had the right to make its own choices about its jurors. One of the Scottsboro Boys, Williams, was allowed a new trial. Williams had been tried as an adult. But he was just 13 years old. The court ruled that this was not fair.

Lawyer Samuel Leibowitz, *left*, defended Patterson, *right*, and other Scottsboro Boys during their appeals trials.

Guards escorted the Scottsboro Boys from jails to courtrooms for their trials.

The Scottsboro Boys' lawyers then appealed their cases to the US Supreme Court. Victory did not seem likely. The lawyers argued that their clients were entitled to a legal defense and had not received one in their initial trials. That was true, but the Supreme Court had never overturned a sentence for that reason before.

In November 1932, the Supreme Court ruled that the young men had not been given access to a legal defense. The Scottsboro cases were sent back to a lower court for further trials. During Patterson's second trial in April 1933, Bates again testified. But this time, her testimony was different. She confessed that she had not been raped. Still, the jury decided that Patterson was guilty. Norris was also found guilty again in 1933. Both were once again sentenced to death.

In February 1935, Norris's case was brought to the Supreme Court. The court overturned his verdict on the grounds that Alabama had not allowed black people to be part of the jury. But he would be found guilty again in another trial just two years later. He was again

HAYWOOD PATTERSON

Haywood Patterson spent much of his life in prison. He was tried four different times for the alleged rape of Price and Bates. He was sentenced to death three times. In 1941 a prison guard paid another inmate to kill Patterson. The inmate stabbed Patterson. But Patterson survived. He later escaped from prison in 1948. His autobiography was published in 1950. He died of cancer two years later.

TRIALS TIMELINE

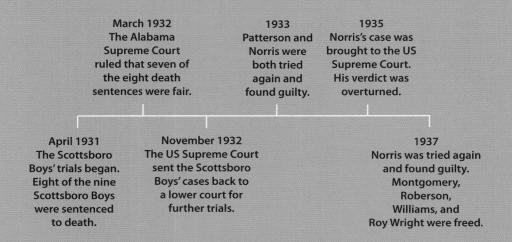

March 1932
The Alabama Supreme Court ruled that seven of the eight death sentences were fair.

1933
Patterson and Norris were both tried again and found guilty.

1935
Norris's case was brought to the US Supreme Court. His verdict was overturned.

April 1931
The Scottsboro Boys' trials began. Eight of the nine Scottsboro Boys were sentenced to death.

November 1932
The US Supreme Court sent the Scottsboro Boys' cases back to a lower court for further trials.

1937
Norris was tried again and found guilty. Montgomery, Roberson, Williams, and Roy Wright were freed.

The above timeline shows key events in the Scottsboro Boys' trials. How do you think the young men's experiences would have been different if they had not gotten help from the ILD? How do you think their experiences would have been different if they had been white defendants?

sentenced to death. Trials for other Scottsboro Boys also continued. Patterson went through another trial in January 1936. His sentence was reduced to 75 years in prison.

In July 1937, the charges against four of the Scottsboro Boys were dropped. Montgomery, Roberson, Williams, and Roy Wright were freed. But the

Lawyer Samuel Leibowitz, *right*, talks with the four Scottsboro Boys who were freed in 1937.

others remained in prison. Andy Wright had also been found guilty again and was sentenced to 99 years in prison. In 1938 the governor of Alabama reduced Norris's sentence from execution to life in prison.

AFTERMATH

None of the Scottsboro Boys ended up serving their full jail sentences. But none of them were released from prison right away either. Even after their releases, the years of trials and imprisonment took their toll on the young men. Most of them left their families behind to start new lives in other parts of the country. Most also kept low profiles because of the constant threat of lynching. They didn't become well-known activists. They avoided talking to the press about their experiences.

Norris was released from prison in 1946. Andy was the last of the Scottsboro Boys to leave prison. He was released in 1950. He had spent nearly 20 years in prison for a crime he did not commit. His brother, Roy, was one of the first Scottsboro Boys to be released in 1937.

But even Roy had spent all of his teen years in prison. Roy struggled to adapt to life after imprisonment. He committed suicide in 1959.

Norris and Patterson later published autobiographies about their experiences. After his release, Montgomery tried unsuccessfully to make a living as a musician. Many of the Scottsboro Boys couldn't pursue their dreams because of their time in prison and the effects it had on them. None of them ever fully recovered from their ordeal.

EXPLORE ONLINE

Chapter Four discusses what happened to the Scottsboro Boys after their trials. The website below goes into more depth on this topic. How is the information from the website the same as the information in this chapter? What new information did you learn from the website?

WHO WERE THE SCOTTSBORO BOYS?
abdocorelibrary.com/scottsboro-boys

ECHOES OF SCOTTSBORO

The Supreme Court rulings in the Scottsboro Boys' trials made life easier for future generations. The Scottsboro Boys' trials helped push the Supreme Court to guarantee a defendant's right to a lawyer. But today, black men still face violence and unfair arrests.

THE JENA SIX

In 2005 Hurricane Katrina displaced thousands of black residents in New Orleans, Louisiana. Many people moved to other states. Others settled in nearby majority-white communities in Louisiana. This resettlement sometimes led

A black teenager lights candles in memory of the Scottsboro Boys during a ceremony in 2013.

PARDONS

For decades after their trials, Alabama still listed three of the Scottsboro Boys as convicted felons. Patterson, Weems, and Andy Wright died before being granted an official pardon by the state. Alabama's parole board finally pardoned them in 2013. Only then did the state acknowledge their innocence.

to tension between white and black people in these communities. One of these communities was the town of Jena.

In August 2006, six black teenagers clashed with a group of white teenagers in Jena. The white teenagers had been bullying the black teenagers for weeks. The black teenagers fought back against one of the bullies on a high school playground. His injuries were minor. Still, the local white prosecutor wanted to make an example of the black teenagers. He charged them with attempted murder. He threatened to imprison them for up to 100 years each. Civil rights activists were outraged. Thousands of people marched in Jena, demanding justice. Meanwhile, some people

Activists protested the imprisonment of the Jena Six in 2007.

published the Jena Six's home addresses online. They threatened the Jena Six. Unlike in the case of the Scottsboro Boys, public pressure alone was enough to force the prosecutor to reduce the charges. Only one of the six black teenagers spent any time in jail.

NEVER INNOCENT ENOUGH

In 1989 a woman was raped in New York City's Central Park. Five teenagers were convicted of the crime. Four of the teenagers were African American. One was Latino. The police questioned the young men for hours. Under this pressure, the young men confessed to a crime they had not committed. The details in their confessions did not match up. But the young men were all convicted. In 2002 the real rapist confessed. DNA evidence confirmed that he was telling the truth. The young men were released. Still, some people refused to believe the young men had not committed the rape. Many people noted the similarities between the experiences of these young men and those of the Scottsboro Boys.

BLACK LIVES MATTER

In February 2012, 17-year-old Trayvon Martin was walking in the majority-white neighborhood of Sanford, Florida. Trayvon was a black teenager. Neighborhood resident George Zimmerman spotted Trayvon and called the police. Zimmerman told police that he thought Trayvon looked suspicious. He confronted Trayvon and shot him to death.

IMPRISONMENT BY RACE

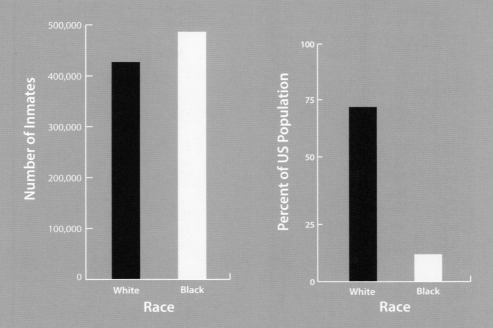

The above graphs show the number of white and black inmates in the United States in 2016 compared to the percent of white and black people in the US population. Why do you think black people continue to be imprisoned at a higher rate than white people?

Zimmerman was later brought to trial. He claimed that he shot Trayvon in self-defense. But Trayvon had been unarmed. Still, the jury found Zimmerman not guilty. He was not sentenced to any jail time. The case and its aftermath reminded people of the injustices African Americans continue to encounter today.

Black Lives Matter activists continue to fight discrimination today.

Each year hundreds of black youths are killed under suspicious circumstances. These killings are not usually considered lynchings because they are often committed by one person. But they show how black people today still encounter many of the problems the Scottsboro Boys faced. Black teenagers still experience violence and injustice, both at the hands of white extremist groups and at the hands of a criminal justice system that continues to sentence them more harshly than their white peers.

The Black Lives Matter movement fights discrimination and works to reduce violence against black people. Three African American women started this movement in 2013 after Zimmerman was found not guilty. Black Lives Matter also works to make sure that those who kill black people are held accountable. Its primary goal is to save the lives of young black people who face the same problems the Scottsboro Boys faced many years ago.

FURTHER EVIDENCE

Chapter Five explores the legacy of the Scottsboro Boys' trials and the challenges African Americans still face today. What was one of the main points of this chapter? What evidence is included to support this point? Visit the website below. Does the information on the website support this point? Does it present new evidence?

AFRICAN AMERICAN HISTORY
abdocorelibrary.com/scottsboro-boys

FAST FACTS

- The Scottsboro Boys were nine black teenagers. They were arrested in Alabama in March 1931. They were charged with assault after they got into a fight with a group of white men. They were later falsely charged with rape.

- The Scottsboro Boys were tried in a series of unfair and rushed trials. Eight of the nine Scottsboro Boys were sentenced to death.

- The US Supreme Court ruled in November 1932 that the Scottsboro Boys had not been given access to a legal defense in their initial trials.

- In February 1935, the Supreme Court overturned Clarence Norris's verdict because Alabama had not allowed black people to be part of the jury.

- The last three Scottsboro Boys to be pardoned were Haywood Patterson, Charles Weems, and Andrew Wright. They were finally pardoned in 2013.

- The Supreme Court rulings in the Scottsboro appeals trials still protect the rights of defendants today.

- Today, the Black Lives Matter movement and civil rights activists continue to bring attention to injustices against African Americans.

STOP AND THINK

Surprise Me

Chapter Three discusses the Scottsboro Boys' trials. After reading this book, what two or three facts about the trials did you find most surprising? Write a few sentences about each fact. Why did you find each fact surprising?

Dig Deeper

After reading this book, what questions do you still have about the Scottsboro Boys? With an adult's help, find a few reliable sources that can help you answer your questions. Write a paragraph about what you learned.

Another View

Chapter Four discusses what happened to the Scottsboro Boys after their trials. As you know, every source is different. Ask a librarian or another adult to help you find another source about this topic. Write a short essay comparing the new source's point of view with that of this book's authors. What is the point of view of each source? How are they different and why?

GLOSSARY

appeal
an attempt to overturn a court's ruling by retrying a case in a higher court, such as the US Supreme Court

defendant
someone who has been accused of a crime

discrimination
the unjust treatment of a person or group based on race or other perceived differences

juror
someone who is a part of a jury, a group that decides a defendant's guilt or innocence in court

pardon
an official statement by a government official declaring someone innocent or forgiven

prosecutor
a lawyer who tries to prove that someone accused of a crime is guilty

rabbi
a person who is trained in Jewish law and who can lead Jewish ceremonies and services

segregation
the separation of people of different races or ethnic groups through separate schools and other public spaces

ONLINE RESOURCES

To learn more about the Scottsboro Boys, visit our free resource websites below.

Visit **abdocorelibrary.com** for free Common Core resources for teachers and students, including vetted activities, multimedia, and booklinks, for deeper subject comprehension.

Visit **abdobooklinks.com** for free additional online weblinks for further learning. These links are routinely monitored and updated to provide the most current information available.

LEARN MORE

Harris, Duchess. *Black Lives Matter*. Minneapolis, MN: Abdo Publishing Company, 2018.

Muldoon, Kathleen M. *The Jim Crow Era*. Minneapolis, MN: Abdo Publishing Company, 2015.

ABOUT THE
AUTHORS

Duchess Harris, JD, PhD

Professor Harris is the chair of the American Studies department at Macalester College and curator of the Duchess Harris Collection of ABDO books. She is the author and coauthor of recently released ABDO books including *Hidden Human Computers: The Black Women of NASA*, *Black Lives Matter*, and *Race and Policing*.

Before working with ABDO, she authored several other books on the topics of race, culture, and American history. She served as an associate editor for *Litigation News*, the American Bar Association Section of Litigation's quarterly flagship publication, and was the first editor in chief of *Law Raza*, an interactive online journal covering race and the law, published at William Mitchell College of Law. She has earned a PhD in American Studies from the University of Minnesota and a JD from William Mitchell College of Law.

Tom Head

Tom Head is author or coauthor of more than 30 nonfiction books, including *World History 101* and *Civil Liberties: A Beginner's Guide*. He holds a PhD in religion and society from Edith Cowan University and is a lifelong resident of Jackson, Mississippi.

INDEX